The
Prairie Dog

Published by Raintree Steck-Vaughn Publishers, an imprint of Steck-Vaughn Company.

Acknowledgments
Project Editor: Helene Resky
Design Manager: Joyce Spicer
Consulting Editor: Kim Merlino
Consultant: Michael Chinery
Illustrated by Graham Allen
Designed by Ian Winton and Steve Prosser
Electronic Cover Production: Alan Klemp
Additional Electronic Production: Bo McKinney and Scott Melcer
Photography credits on page 32

Planned and produced by The Creative Publishing Company

Library of Congress Cataloging-in-Publication Data
> Crewe, Sabrina
> The prairie dog / Sabrina Crewe ; [illustrated by Graham Allen].
>   p.   cm. — (Life cycles)
> Includes index.
>   Summary: Describes the life cycle, behavior, and habitat of the members of the squirrel family that live in underground burrows.
>   ISBN 0-8172-4365-8 (hardcover). — ISBN 0-8172-6228-8 (pbk.)
>   1. Prairie dogs — Juvenile literature.   2. Cynomys ludovicianus — Juvenile literature.   3. Prairie dogs — Life cycles — Juvenile literature.   4. Cynomys ludovicianus — Life cycles — Juvenile literature.   [1. Prairie dogs.]   I. Allen, Graham, 1940- .   II. Title.   III. Series: Crewe, Sabrina. Life cycles.
> QL737.R68C74   1997
> 599.32'32 — dc20
>   96-4828
>   CIP   AC

1 2 3 4 5 6 7 8 9 0 LB 00 99 98 97 96
Printed and bound in the United States of America.

Words explained in the glossary appear in **bold** the first time they are used in the text.

The
Prairie Dog

Sabrina Crewe

RSVP

RAINTREE
STECK-VAUGHN
P U B L I S H E R S
The Steck-Vaughn Company

Austin, Texas

The prairie dogs are under the ground.

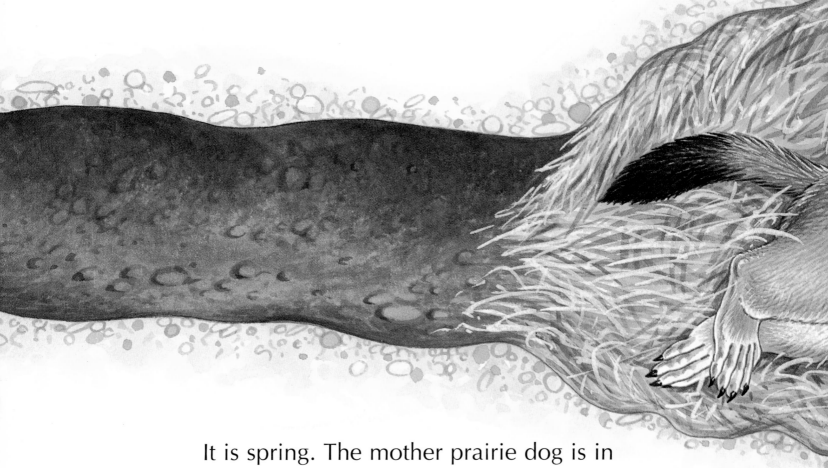

It is spring. The mother prairie dog is in
her **burrow**. She has a new **litter** of pups.
The pups are very tiny. They feed on milk
from their mother.

There are four pups.

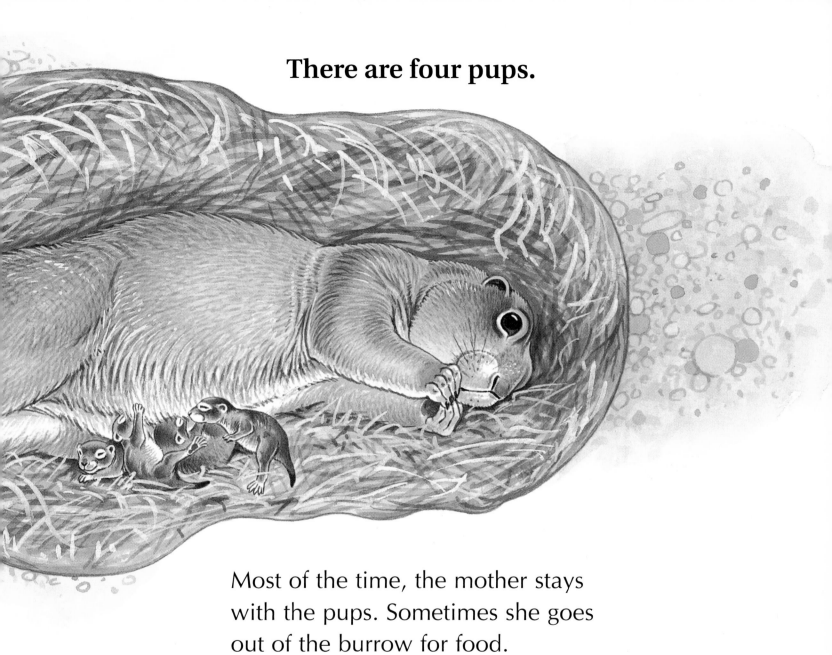

Most of the time, the mother stays
with the pups. Sometimes she goes
out of the burrow for food.

The pups are five weeks old.

The pups have grown quickly. Now
they can open their eyes. They have
not been out of the burrow yet.

The pups are coming out of the burrow.

The pups are six weeks old. They
are ready to go out of the burrow
and look around.

The mother keeps careful watch.

When the pups are small, they stay
close to their mother. She still **nurses**
them when they first leave the burrow.
But soon the pups start to eat plants, too.

The pup is eating grass.

Prairie dogs bite blades of grass with their front teeth. Then they hold the grass in their paws and nibble it.

The prairie dogs live in a town.

A prairie dog town covers a big area of **grassland**. You can tell a prairie dog town by the short grass and many **mounds** of soil. Thousands of prairie dogs can live in one town.

Living in a large group helps protect
prairie dogs. There are many prairie
dogs watching and listening for danger
every moment. This makes it hard for
predators to catch them.

The town has many mounds.

The mounds of soil are the openings into the prairie dogs' burrows. Each burrow has at least two openings. Under the ground, there are long tunnels leading to small **chambers**.

The burrow is a family home.

Each group of burrows is the home of
a **coterie**. There are several females
and pups in a coterie. Every coterie also
has one adult male. When the pups are
outside the burrow, all the adults in the
coterie help to watch them.

The prairie dogs greet each other.

Prairie dogs touch noses when they meet.
This helps them **identify** members of their
own coterie.

The pups play together.

As the pups get bigger, they play with the
other pups in their coterie. They don't stay
so close to their mother anymore.

The prairie dog is fully grown.

Prairie dogs become adults when they are
one year old. The male prairie dog has left
his family to form his own coterie. He makes
a new burrow at the edge of the town.

The prairie dog has a muddy nose.

Prairie dogs use their front paws to
dig their burrows. Then they use their
noses to pat everything into shape!

The prairie dog is on guard.

The male in the coterie is always **alert.** He protects his **territory** while the rest of the group eat. He gives a warning bark if he senses danger.

Coyotes are enemies.

A **coyote** has come to the town to hunt prairie dogs. The prairie dogs have heard the warning. They disappear quickly under the ground.

The prairie dog is barking.

The prairie dog stands on its back legs and calls loudly. Its bark is a sign that the danger is over. It tells the other prairie dogs it is safe to come out.

Winter has come.

The prairie dogs are much fatter. The fat on their bodies will keep them warm and provide them with food during the winter. They have stored some food in their burrow, too.

The prairie dogs stay in their burrow.

In winter, prairie dogs spend most
of the time under the ground. They
sleep through the coldest weather
to save energy.

Prairie dogs are ready to mate
when they are one or two years
old. They mate in their burrows
during the winter.

The prairie dog is making a nest.

In early spring, the female gathers dried plants. She takes them into her burrow. She makes a nest in the chamber where she will have her pups. She stays by herself until the pups are born.

Prairie dogs need prairies.

Much of the grassland where prairie
dogs lived is now farmland or land for
cattle. Many prairie dog towns have been
destroyed. People can help prairie dogs
by protecting the wild prairies where
they make their homes.

The Burrow of a Prairie Dog

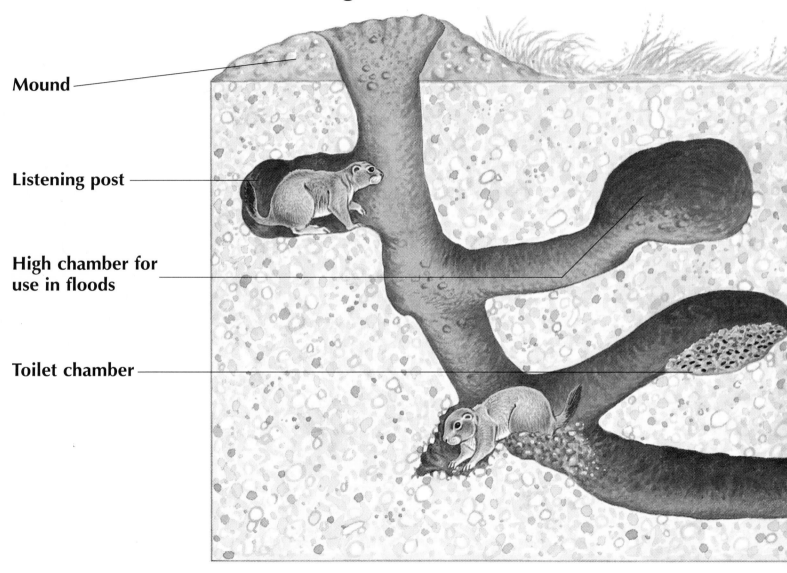

Mound

Listening post

High chamber for use in floods

Toilet chamber

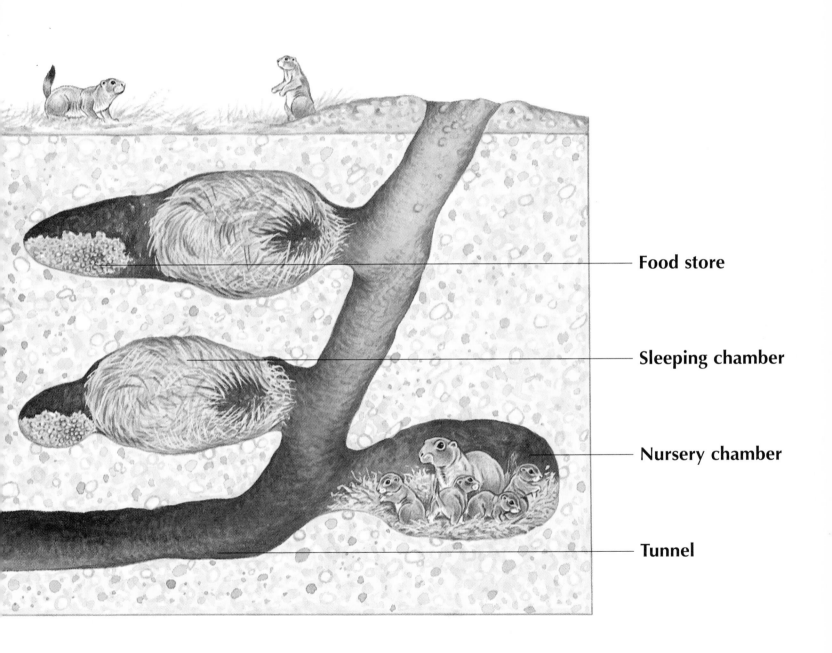

Food store

Sleeping chamber

Nursery chamber

Tunnel

Prairie dogs are rodents.

Rodents are a type of **mammal** with four gnawing teeth at the front of their mouths. Prairie dogs are not dogs at all but members of the squirrel family. The prairie dog in this book is a black-tailed prairie dog. Here is another prairie dog and some other kinds of rodents.

White-tailed prairie dog

Porcupine

Gerbil

Deer mouse

28

Red squirrel

Beaver

Wood rat

Guinea pig

Where the Black-Tailed Prairie Dog Lives

Alaska

CANADA

UNITED
STATES

Areas where
the black-tailed
prairie dog lives

MEXICO

Glossary

Alert Watching out for danger

Burrow A hole or tunnel made in the ground by an animal

Chamber A room

Coterie A family group of prairie dogs

Coyote A wild dog

Grassland An area of land mostly covered in grass

Identify To know who or what something is

Litter A group of young animals born together from the same mother

Mammal A kind of animal that usually has fur and feeds its young with milk

Mound A pile of soil

Nurse To feed young animals with mother's milk

Predator An animal that hunts and kills other animals for food

Rodent A type of mammal with four gnawing teeth at the front of its mouth

Territory An area of land that an animal defends as its own

Index